The Writer in the Garden

Roger Evans

THE BRITISH LIBRARY

Introduction

'God Almighty first planted a garden: and indeed it is the purest of human pleasures. It is the greatest refreshment of the spirits of man'. The familiar opening sentences of Francis Bacon's essay *Of Gardens* echo the *Book of Genesis*: 'And the Lord God planted a garden east-ward in Eden; and there he put the man whom he had formed.'

All gardens are to some degree recreations of the Garden of Eden, established by God as the first home of Man before the Fall, and we might say that gardening was therefore Man's first work. And Woman's also, according to Milton in whose imagination Eve was actually gardening – tying up roses – when the Serpent came upon her.

To the medieval mind, the idea of a terrestrial paradise was a reality and it is quite firmly represented on the early twelfth-century map of the world that opens this book. Outside the Garden there is a fearful wilderness. The garden in the fourteenth-century poem *Pearl* must have been a great comfort to the speaker in that lovely work: a man in mourning for his dead child, he miraculously finds her in that haven of a place. But, of course, it is a dream and the vision may have many layers of significance.

Le Roman de la Rose, from the thirteenth century, is also a dream-poem and in its presentation of courtly love it embraces Christian ideals but by the end of the fifteenth century, when the Flemish illumination shown in this book (p. 8) was made, the garden's association with sensuous pleasures – erotic ones in particular – was fully developed.

In Tudor England, the rise of the favourite in court, the creation of a new aristocratic class and the establishment of powerful patrons, all conspired to create gardens of considerable size and of dazzling complexity that demanded much labour. Thus emerged remarkable men like John Gerard, head gardener to Lord Burghley at Theobalds, an avid searcher of new plants and a man endowed with that facility of language that marks a writer of note. Francis Bacon was weighted with onerous affairs of state, but nevertheless worked lovingly, even passionately, in his gardens, deeply concerned with recovering knowledge lost with the Fall and the Flood. We may stand in what was his old garden in Gray's Inn and muse on its loss again.

By no means prepared to be whimsical in their theology, some seventeenth-century writers such as Donne and Milton remind us of the dark side of Eden, the presence in it of Evil. The speaker in Donne's poem 'Twicknam Garden' regrets that he destroys the garden's peace by his bringing the Serpent into the garden with him and Milton's *Paradise Lost* faces the problem of Evil head on.

We find little such disturbance in the work of Milton's contemporary, the diarist John Evelyn, however. Gardening for him was a labour 'full of tranquillity and satisfaction'. He had mounted as a motto above his door: '*Intret in has aedas nil nisi tuta quies*' (May nothing enter this house but complete peace). In the act of gardening the active life was, for him, reconciled with the contemplative life, so that the whole garden became suffused with meaning; it was a 'mysterie', a metaphor for what was passionate or tender. Of all our writers, he was one of the most deeply engaged in the practice and theory of gardening.

The great gardens of the latter end of the seventeenth century were highly formal with spacious parterres and clipped trees and hedges, all geometrically precise in arrangement, all expressing the notion of Man's benign dominance over Nature. By the second quarter of the eighteenth century, however, gardens were beginning to represent a quite different idea about the natural world. With advances in scientific and geological knowledge, earlier explanations of the history and structure of the world became superseded, and complex geometric gardens, which had derived from the earlier notion, became drained of meaning. The natural landscape was no longer perceived as a wilderness, but as possessing a 'genuine order' in its own right, in itself expressing the presence of God.

Writers from this period, such as Pope and Thomson, were at the forefront in expressing this view. Pope's ideal: 'First follow Nature, and your judgment frame/By her just standard…' was picked up and modified by garden designers such as William Kent who 'leaped the fence and saw that all nature was a garden'. The interaction between poet (Pope), painter, landscape designer, architect (Kent was all three) and wealthy patron (the Earl of Burlington) was an immensely influential one in the first half of the eighteenth century. This period proved to be one of those galvanising eras of change. It was not by chance that Kent, aglow with his recent Continental exploration of the pictures of Claude and Poussin, should illustrate Thomson's *The Seasons* with Arcadian vistas.

The concept of 'Nature', however, changed in the course of the eighteenth century. The composed landscape arranged as in a picture (a kind of vegetable flourish sitting on a mineral one) was not enough for later

sensibilities. The poet William Shenstone wanted his woods and streams to convey associations of mind – a melancholy spinney here and a cheerful rivulet there – to evoke a heightened poetic awareness, ignoring the fact that his *ferme ornée* was really a very shabby old farmhouse that he neglected shamefully.

Such developments in how Nature was viewed led to those extremes of artificially created savageness that Dr Johnson observed with awe at the Hawkestone estate and Richard Graves dwelt on with relish in his novel *Columella*. The naturalist, Gilbert White, with his fastidious attention to tiny detail, an attention worthy of a man of the cloth who venerated the Creation, would have had no sympathy with such grandiose ideas, just as the generation of notable poets, emerging as the eighteenth century drew to a close, were less interested in artificial effects than in their own personal responses to the world.

By the nineteenth century, the sense that gardens could express important ideas about the natural world was being dissipated by changing social patterns. The vast population shift into towns and cities and the economic preoccupations of a developing middle class had a far-reaching effect on garden design. John Claudius Loudon and his wife Jane caught the tide and, through their highly influential publications, became leading exponents of what has been called 'the gardenesque', creating villa gardens that displayed the gardener's skills. Such showy gardens became ideal solutions for municipal authorities intent on improving their purlieus, and public parks – today mere spindly shades of their former selves – were the result.

Left Sunflower from a manuscript book of herbs, flowers and trees, 1684. Add. MS 5282, f. 25.

Above From *Gardening for Children*, 1848, by the Revd. C. A. Johns, following in the footsteps of Jane Loudon's *Gardening for Ladies*, 1841. 7055. a. 32.

The scientific examination of particular species of garden plants had been part of the life work of John Evelyn but the nineteenth century was massively industrious in this field: it promoted such examination but also disseminated the accumulated information. A driving force was the Horticultural Society founded in 1804 (it became Royal in 1861) and we find many new plants being introduced into Britain – fuchsias from South America in the 1820s and hybrid rhododendrons from North America soon afterwards. Edward Lear's minor experiments with varieties of Ipomoea in his San Remo garden were typical, his seeds coming not only from India but also from Sir John Lubbock's garden at Downe in Kent.

For the imagination, the concept of a garden can be a richly creative force. What Victorian writers such as Tennyson or Morris or Swinburne make of the concept is often disturbing. The garden in Tennyson's *Maud* is one that exists in a dark layer of the mind: it is erotic; it is dangerous. The opening lines of the poem set the tone:

> I hate the dreadful hollow behind the
>   little wood,
> Its lips in the field above are dabbled
>   with blood-red heath…

But the concept of a garden can also be enchanting and enchantment is a vital force in children's literature. Walter Crane's re-telling of old tales, his processions of bright, spirited garden flowers and evocative organic designs were very consciously crafted to help children to read, so that a strong moral purpose joins forces with the imagination in work like his. There is still a sense of the moral value of a garden in Frances Hodgson Burnett's work, *The Secret Garden*, but appearing as it does in that late Edwardian twilight in 1911, it also has a nostalgic quality. It reflects on a garden that once was, is now a ruin and can be given life again.

A ruin is what Edward Thomas's garden is in his little, untitled, poem of 1915. In the midst of the terrible conflict of the First World War, the vision of Paradise for those at the front must have faded to nothing behind the horror of the blasted trees and bloated corpses, but the struggle of Thomas's periwinkle gives hope that the generation can somehow hang on. Laurence Binyon, writing in the Second World War, bestows upon his orchard the same quality when he thinks of 'other Junes than ours'.

Whether the human spirit can always maintain this kind of optimism is, of course, another matter. Enchantment can become disenchantment. Katherine Mansfield's interwar *Suburban Fairy Tale* picks up this thread and the barren little plot in which she so caustically sets her story bespeaks garden-apathy.

From such moral and cultural lowlands it was a struggle for the nation to rise up again. By 1945 what was left of Europe looked around exhausted and saw a wasteland. In 1951, the holding of the Festival of Britain and, in 1962, the consecration of the rebuilt Coventry Cathedral expressed the national need for tangible signs of recovery, but few things accomplished that so victoriously and movingly as Vita Sackville-West's white garden, begun in 1949 at Sissinghurst. From what was once an abandoned wilderness, she and her husband created a living garden. It might, as a whole, have taken twenty years to do it, but that garden rose from the dead.

With a society bereft of the ideals and influences of institutions that had increasingly little part to play in many people's lives, the later twentieth century found itself turned in upon itself with self-doubt, irresolution and even distress. Sir Michael Tippett's opera *The Knot Garden* of 1970 expresses that, but the allotments of Melvyn Bragg's novel *Crystal Rooms* are positively restorative, a cure for social as well as emotional ills. In this plot of land by the railway lines, among the blowsy peonies, we are not far from Andrew Marvell's 'green Thought', not far from John Evelyn's 'best representation of our lost felicitie'.

If the present-day reader may feel that this Edenic image of our 'lost felicitie' is an anachronism and that we have travelled far from that simple garden placed 'east-ward' on the map that opens this book, it is worth looking back to Milton to see exactly what he means by 'Paradise'.

In Book XII of *Paradise Lost*, the Archangel Michael addresses Adam, saying that even if Man achieves complete knowledge of 'all the ethereal powers/All secrets of the deep, all nature's works', then it is to his own benefit to:

> add faith,
> Add virtue, patience, temperance, add love
> By name to come called Charity, the soul
> Of all the rest: then wilt thou not be loath
> To leave this Paradise, but shalt possess
> A paradise within thee, happier far.

Even ignoring the redemptive nature of that declaration, there is a valuable truth here. Many a gardener, applying the thought to his or her own labours, will recognise that truth. For many of the writers in this book it was a truth worth wrestling with.

Left Walter Crane, *A Floral Fantasy in an Old English Garden*, 1899. Front cover. 11651. l. 47.

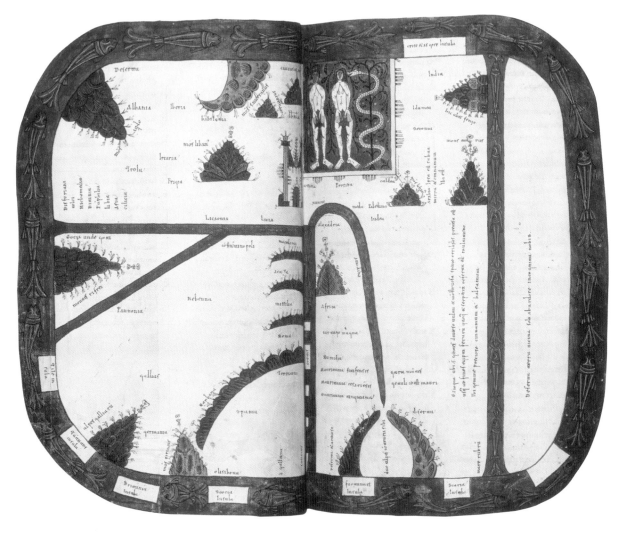

Silos Beatus

The Garden of Eden is clearly shown on the Beatus Maps of the World. Saint Beatus, a Benedictine monk of Liébana in northern Spain, created the prototype of the genre in AD 776 with his cartographic illustration to the *Book of Revelation*. About fourteen copies of the map, by other hands, dating from the eighth to the thirteenth centuries, are known to have survived.

The one illustrated here is dated 1109. It provokes thought. Seemingly imprecise in its location (east is at the top of the map), how solidly precise the palisaded Garden is and how firm the delineation of details within it, such as fingers, toes and forbidden fruit! In contrast the world outside seems fluid and uncertain. It tells us that, having fallen and having been cast out, Mankind loses the security and peace the Garden provided.

Above The Silos Beatus Map of the World, 1109. Add. MS 11695, ff. 39v–40.

Pearl

Early interpretations of this late-fourteenth-century anonymous poem saw the speaker as a man in mourning for his daughter, the Pearl, who dies aged two, and the garden he lies in as a Garden of Remembrance. Recent commentators, with a broader view of the medieval mind, see the Pearl as an allegorical figure, a symbol of Purity, even Christ or a state of grace.

The garden has an earthly reality, however. It is described as an *erber* (arbour). This may be greensward or it may be a herb garden and the plants described are both medicinal and, through their fragrance, narcotic and trance-inducing.

Le Roman de la Rose

The thirteenth-century French poem *Le Roman de la Rose* was hugely popular and well disseminated in manuscript form. The first part, of some four thousand or more lines, is a dream sequence experienced by a lusty young man in the amorous month of May. He sets out to find the Rose, symbolic of romantic love, and finds himself outside a walled garden, the Garden of Pleasure. He is let in by Lady Idleness.

Here is the scene in a late-fourteenth-century translation attributed to Geoffrey Chaucer:

And forth withoute wordis mo
In at the wiket went I tho
That ydelnesse hadde opened me
Into that gardyne faire to see
And when I was Inne Iwys[1]
Myn herte was ful glad of this
For wel wende I ful sikerly[2]
Haue ben in paradys erthly
So faire it was that trusteth wel
It semede a place espirituel
For certys as at my deuys[3]
Ther is no place in paradys
So good Inne forto dwelle or be
As in that gardyne thought me
For there was many abridde syngyng
Thorough out the yerde al thringyng[4]
In many places were nyghtyngales
Alpes fynches and wodewales[5]

1 inside
2 believed truly
3 as it seemed to me
4 gathering
5 Bullfinches/
   woodpeckers

The illustrated image of the garden is from a late-fifteenth-century Flemish manuscript which provides details of the courtly *herber*, the little enclosed garden with a fountain set on a lawn and with surrounding banks surmounted by turf and trellis work.

Left The Garden of Pleasure, showing the dreamer being admitted. From a late-fifteenth-century Flemish manuscript of *Le Roman de la Rose*. Harley MS 4425, f. 12v.

John Gerard

In 1596 John Gerard published what was the first list of the contents of a garden, his own quite small garden in Holborn, London (on the south side of the highway, possibly at the juncture with Fetter Lane, where, in the twenty-first century, steel and glass now tower). For some twenty years he had been an avid collector, both here and abroad, of new and interesting plants, not only for his own plot – where he was the first person to grow potatoes in this country – but also for the great estate of his master, Lord Burghley, Theobalds in Hertfordshire.

At the beginning of Gerard's *Herball*, published in 1597, he speaks with undying vibrancy of his horticultural efforts in his address to Burghley, who was Lord High Treasurer of England:

> To the large and singular furniture of this noble Island I have added from forreine places all the varietie of herbes and floures that I might any way obtaine, I have laboured with the soile to make it fit for plants, and with the plants, that they might delight in the soile, that so they might live and prosper under our clymat, as in their native and proper countrey: what my successe hath beene, and what my furniture is, I leave to the report of they that have seene your Lordships gardens, and the little plot of myne owne especiall care and husbandry.

With disarming charm, Gerard noted in his garden catalogue the precise spots where his plants were found. Of the Hooded Willow Herbe (*Lysimachia galericulata*) he says, 'This I found in a waterie lane leading from the Lord Treasurers House called Thibals unto the backside of his slaughter house'. This map, dated 1611, of the great Theobalds' estate is but a shadowy glimpse of the house's past glory.

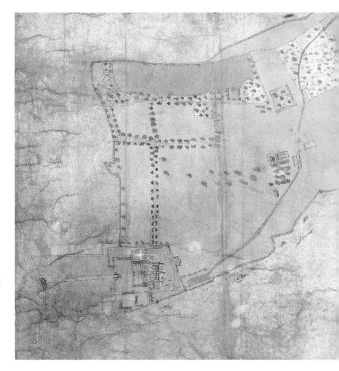

Right Detail from a manuscript map by the great architect John Thorpe of Theobalds, Lord Burghley's estate in Hertfordshire, dated 1611. Cotton MS Augustus I. i.75.

> *Twicknam Garden:*
>
> Blasted with Sighes and surrounded with teares,
>   hither I come, to seeke the Springe.
> And at mine eyes and at myne eares,
>   Receiue such balme as els cures eury thinge.
>   But oh Selfe traytor I doe bringe
> The Spider Loue, which transubstantiates all
> And can conuert Manna to Gall.
>   And that this place may thoroughlie be thought
>   True Paradise, I haue the Serpent brought.
>
> Twere holsomer for me, that winter did
>   Benight the glory of this place.
> And that a gray frost did forbid
>   These trees to laughe, and mocke me to my face
>   But that I may not this disgrace
> Indure, nor leaue this Garden (Loue) let me
> Some senceles peece of this place bee
>   Make me a mandrake So I may growe here
>   Or a stone fountaine, weepinge out the yeare
>
> Hither with Christall vialls (Louers) come
>   And take my teares, which are Loues wine
> And try your Mistres teares at home.
>   For all are false which taste not iust like mine
>   Alas, hartes doe not in me eyes shine
> Nor can you more iudge womens thoughts by teares:
> Then by hir shadowe what she weares
>   O peruerse Sex where none is true but she
>   Who's therefore true because hir truthe kills me

Left A transcript of John Donne's 'Twicknam Garden' in an unknown early-seventeenth-century hand. Stowe MS 961, f. 87.

John Donne

Between 1607 and 1617, Twickenham Park was leased to Lucy, Countess of Bedford, closest friend of James I's consort and a dazzlingly influential woman in her time. The estate had previously been leased to Francis Bacon and no doubt a Baconian hand could be seen in the garden design.

In about 1607, she met, and became patroness of, John Donne, by then a married man of thirty-five, she herself some thirteen years married. There was much mutual respect between them and no suggestion at all of adulterous intimacy.

The poem 'Twicknam Garden', written c.1607, is not an address by Donne in simple autobiographical form. Here he adopts the *persona* of a lover who, following a convention, falls into dejection in spring time, for his love is hopeless. The garden is made 'True Paradise' only insofar as he has brought the Serpent, in the form of 'The Spider Love', into the garden with him. It is a melancholy comment on love's malign powers and the 'gray frost' will find a melancholy echo later in this book.

OF GARDENS. AN ESSAY BY FRANCIS LORD BACON.

GOD ALMIGHTY FIRST PLANTED A GARDEN: AND INDEED IT IS THE PUREST OF HUMAN PLEASURES. IT IS the GREATEST REFRESHMENT OF THE SPIRITS OF MAN; without WHICH, BUILDINGS & PALACES ARE BUT GROSS HANDYWORKS: AND A MAN SHALL EVER See, THAT WHEN AGES GROW TO CIVILITY & ELEGANCY, MEN COME TO BUILD STATELY, SOONER than TO GARDEN FINELY, as if GARDENING WERE THE GREATER PERFECTION. I DO HOLD IT, IN THE ROYAL ORDERING OF GARDENS, THERE OUGHT to BE GARDENS FOR ALL THE MONTHS IN the YEAR: IN WHICH, SEVERALLY, THINGS of BEAUTY MAY BE THEN IN SEASON. FOR DECEMBER AND JANUARY, & THE LATTER PART of NOVEMBER, YOU must TAKE SUCH THINGS AS ARE GREEN all WINTER; HOLLY, IVY, BAYS, JUNIPER, CYPRESS-trees, YEW, PINE-APPLE Trees, FIR TREES, ROSEMARY,

Francis Bacon

Francis Bacon's famous essay *Of Gardens*, published in 1612, was written in Gray's Inn, London, where he began his lawyer's training in 1576 and where he retained a residence for most of his life. His windows looked out onto the garden which he made, in effect, his own. Extant records show that in 1600 alone he spent £60-6s-8d on its elm, birch and cherry trees, woodbine, eglantine, standard roses, 'pincks, violetts and primroses'.

The beautiful edition illustrated here is that made by Lucien Pissarro, son of the painter Camille Pissarro, in 1902. The lettering was done by Lucien's wife, Esther. Interestingly it was in 1902 that the couple moved to Stamford Brook in London and developed a veritable passion for their garden, exchanging notes about gardening with Monet.

Above The opening of Francis Bacon's *Of Gardens*, 1902.
C. 99. b. 3.

Andrew Marvell

Above Engraved portrait of Marvell and (**below**) extract from 'The Garden', taken from the posthumous first edition of his *Miscellaneous Poems*, 1681, edited, according to the title page, by his widow. In fact, Marvell never married. C. 59. i. 8.

Thomas, Third Baron Fairfax, Commander of the Parliamentary Armies, resigned his position in 1650, possibly as a result of the beheading of Charles I. Oliver Cromwell succeeded him and Fairfax retired to Nun Appleton in Yorkshire. There, in 1651, he hired Andrew Marvell to act as a tutor to his young daughter and Marvell stayed in residence for some two years. It seems probable that his great poem, 'The Garden', was written at Nun Appleton.

The poem is highly complex but its main thread is simple enough: the peace of a garden is to be preferred to the stress of the world outside. Shown here is the sixth of its nine verses, culminating in its most famous line:

> To a green Thought in a green Shade

The drift of the verse is this: my mind withdraws from the lesser pleasures of the senses to the pleasures created *within* the mind, so creating another world; and the visible world is rejected in favour of those innocent thoughts that come to it from a garden setting.

Mean while the Mind, from pleaſure leſs,
Withdraws into its happineſs :
The Mind, that Ocean where each kind
Does ſtreight its own reſemblance find ;
Yet it creates, tranſcending theſe,
Far other Worlds, and other Seas ;
Annihilating all that's made
To a green Thought in a green Shade.

John Evelyn

In 1652 the diarist John Evelyn moved into his wife's family home, Sayes Court, an unexceptional Tudor manor house with a run-down garden whose east wall pressed hard against the Thames dockyards at Deptford. With a consuming passion he set about this misty, unprepossessing spot, creating what was to become 'a little world'.

A garden, he said, is 'the place of all terrestrial enjoyments the most resembling Heaven and the best representation of our lost felicitie' and he saw gardening itself as an activity approaching a state of grace. He built an Italianate formal garden, a nursery, a lake with an island, an orchard of three hundred trees, a laboratory and, his greatest delight, groves of trees ('nature's temples') set among evergreen shrubs. His great work on trees, *Sylva* (1664), is lasting testimony to his intense commitment.

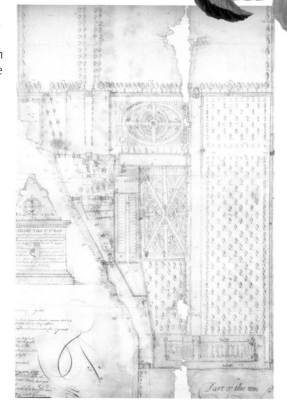

Above Peaches, from a manuscript volume inscribed 'A book containing herbs, flowers and Trees either growing wild or cultivated in gardens in England especially near London in about 1684'. Unknown artist. Add. MS 5282, f. 103.

Right Evelyn's pen-and-ink drawing of garden tools and equipment in his *'Elysium Britannicum'*, an encyclopaedia of gardening which remained unfinished and unpublished. Add. MS 78342, f. 58.

Left Sayes Court, Deptford. Evelyn made this plan soon after moving into the house in 1652. South is at the top. Add. MS 78628A.

43

44

45 46 60

60

broader ralli
at top. 46

47

47

47

48

48

48 C

48

48 C

49

49

50

52

51

51

51

56

56

53

54

reforme this more like a wily dishe:

55

56

56

56

57

50

57

59

60

61

62

63

64

64

65

65

66 A B
Amarill Amilia
8. 6. 16.

67

68

68

69

67

68

69

69

John Milton

John Martin's terrifying engraved image here captures the moment in *Paradise Lost* when Eve takes the fatal step:

   Forth reaching to the fruit, she plucked, she ate

John Milton's words, published in 1667, are in this case as compressed as their counterpart in the *Book of Genesis*, but Milton enriched the surrounding text beyond recognition. The activities of both Adam and Eve before and after the Fall were newly created in his imagination. In the poem, for example, she is alone, gardening, when Satan, in the form of the Serpent, comes upon her:

   Beyond his hope, Eve separate he spies,
   Veiled in a cloud of fragrance, where she stood,
   Half spied, so thick the roses bushing round
   About her glowed, oft stooping to support
   Each flower of slender stalk, whose head though gay
   Carnation, purple, azure, or specked with gold,
   Hung drooping unsustained, them she upstays
   Gently with myrtle band…

Tying up roses is commonplace enough but these roses are by no means commonplace. The word 'carnation' is here used adjectivally with the meaning 'flesh-coloured', a strange colour for the flower but no stranger than 'purple, azure or specked with gold', all quite alien hues in the world of roses. These flowers are splendid, august, baroque – flowers of a world not now known to us.

But what of the world after Eve has taken the irrecoverable step? Adam, awaiting her return, has lovingly made a garland for her head. She goes to him, tells him what she has done and

   From his slack hand the garland wreathed for Eve
   Down dropped, and all the faded roses shed…

'Faded roses': these are the roses we know only too well.

From *The Paradise Lost of Milton with illustrations*, **designed and engraved by John Martin, 2 vols, London 1827. 643. m. 19.**

Alexander Pope

Alexander Pope's garden by the Thames at Twickenham covered five acres, most of it behind the house in the picture shown here. He aimed for simplicity and naturalness. We can see from the illustrated scribbled plans, done on an old letter in about 1720, how he endeavoured to make geometrically angular and straight paths in his garden (as shown on the right-hand plan) more informally sinuous (as shown on the left-hand plan). He was not averse, however, to such artificial creations as a grotto, nor statuary, nor an obelisk (all of which he had), as long as such adornments arose from the 'Genius of the Place' and were not forced upon it.

Pope's ideas found powerful expression in his writing and we can see his stance on garden design in the fragment from his *Epistle to Richard Boyle, Earl of Burlington*, published in 1731. The poem's subject is how the Vanity of Riches can pervert taste but good sense can correct that. Nature herself, he says, is the guide.

Below Pope's plans for paths in his garden, drawn by him on the address panel of a letter addressed to his mother, *c*. 1720. Add. MS 4808, f. 186v.

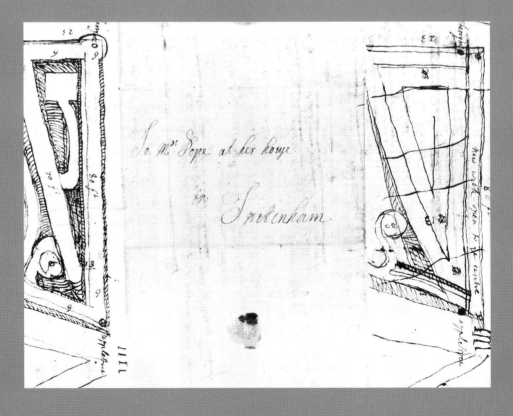

Shall call the winds thro' long Arcades to roar,   35
Proud to catch cold at a *Venetian* door;
Conscious they act a true *Palladian* part,
And if they starve, they starve by rules of art.
   Oft have you hinted to your brother Peer,
A certain truth, which many buy too dear: 40
Something there is, more needful than Expence,
And something previous ev'n to Taste —— 'Tis *Sense*:
Good Sense, which only is the gift of heav'n,
And tho' no science, fairly worth the seven:
A light, which in yourself you must perceive;   45
Jones and *Le Nôtre* have it not to give.
   To build, to plant, whatever you intend,
To rear the Column, or the Arch to bend,
To swell the Terras, or to sink the Grot;
In all let *Nature* never be forgot.   50
But treat the Goddess like a modest fair,
Nor over-dress, nor leave her wholly bare;
Let not each beauty ev'ry where be spy'd,
Where half the skill is decently to hide.

V. 36. A Door or window, so call'd, from being
much practised at Venice, by Palladio and others.
   V. 39, &c. That the first principle and foundation
of all Taste, is *Good Sense.*
   V. 46. *Inigo Jones,* the celebrated Architect, and M.
Le Nôtre, the Designer of the best Gardens of *France.*
   V. 47, &c. The chief proof of good Sense in this,
as in every thing else, is to *follow Nature,* but with
Judgment, and Choice.

He

He gains all points, who *pleasingly confounds,*   55
Surprizes, varies, and conceals the Bounds.
   Consult the *Genius* of the place in all;
That tells the Waters or to rise, or fall,
Or helps th' ambitious Hill the heav'ns to scale,
Or scoops in circling Theatres the Vale,   60
Calls in the Country, catches opening glades,
Joins willing woods, and varies shades from shades;
Now breaks, or now directs, th' intending lines;
Paints as you plant, and as you work, designs.
   Begin with *Sense,* of ev'ry Art the soul,   65
Parts answ'ring parts shall slide into a Whole,
Spontaneous beauties all around advance,
Start ev'n from *Difficulty,* strike from *Chance;*
Nature shall join you, *Time* shall make it grow
A Work to wonder at —— perhaps a STOW.   70
   Without it, proud *Versailles!* thy glory falls,
And *Nero's* Terraces desert their walls:
The vast Parterres a thousand hands shall make,
Lo! COBHAM comes, and floats them with a Lake:

V. 57, &c. The first Rule, to adapt all to the *Nature*
and *Use* of the *Place,* and the beauties not forced into it
but resulting from it.
   V. 70. The Seat and Gardens of the Lord Viscount
Cobham in Buckinghamshire.
   V. 71, &c. For want of this *Sense,* and thro' neglect
of this *Rule,* men are disappointed in the most expensive
undertakings. Nothing without this will ever please
long, if it pleases *at all.*

D   Or

Above Lines 35–74 of Pope's *Epistle to Richard Boyle, Earl of Burlington,* 1731. The marginal corrections are in Pope's hand. C. 122. e. 31.
Left 'An exact Draught and View of Mr Pope's House at Twickenham' by Rysbrack; engraved by Parr, n.d. K. Top. xxx. 19. s.

James Thomson

James Thomson's poem *The Seasons* was published piecemeal first of all: *Winter* in 1726, *Summer* in 1727; *Spring* in 1728. Then, with the support of some very notable subscribers – the Earl of Burlington and Alexander Pope among them – he issued the whole work, including *Autumn* in 1730.

After that he found it difficult to leave it alone and he was easily persuaded to add to and alter the four parts of his creation. In the illustration here, we see Thomson tinkering with *Spring* in 1743. He has taken his 1738 edition, interleaved its pages with blank sheets and made the 'blushing borders' (line 486) of the printed text burgeon with wallflowers, stocks and polyanthus. He is gardening as he writes.

Above A page from Thomson's 1738 edition of *The Seasons* with autograph additions made in 1743. C. 28. e. 17.

William Shenstone

We may remember William Shenstone's mock-Spenserian stanzas in his poem 'The Schoolmistress' (published in 1742) but little else of his amiable, graceful verse. His great creation was really his estate, The Leasowes, situated between Birmingham and Kidderminster.

He began work on the grounds – he neglected the house – in about 1745 and from then until his death in 1763 he followed the landscape designer William Kent's principles of the Picturesque and made the spot one of the major garden attractions of the mid-eighteenth century.

Using one of the sources of the River Stour, which rises in the grounds, Shenstone created tumbling streams with rocky declivities embraced by trees. He artfully adorned nature with Gothic seats, 'Virgil's obelisk', a piping faun, a ruined priory, etc., all formed to sustain, by their associations, states of mind such as contemplation or melancholy. The result was poised somewhere between the natural and the artificial. It was a garden poem.

Above View of the Leasowes and Priory by H. F. James; engraved by Stadler, n.d. K.Top. xxxvi. 21. 3. b.

Samuel Johnson

Samuel Johnson's visit to north Wales in 1774, in the company of his friends Hester and Henry Thrale, is documented in his journal. En route they stopped at Hawkestone, the estate of Sir Rowland Hill, in Shropshire which was already by then a tourist attraction. Indeed a hotel was to be built to accommodate visitors in 1792. Its wildly savage landscape, part of which became known as 'Swisserland', its follies, its grotto and a feature known as 'the Lion's Den' provoked what Johnson calls 'a kind of turbulent pleasure between fright and admiration'.

Though it wants water [he writes], it excels Dovedale by the extent of its prospects, the awfulness of its shades, the horrors of its precipices, the verdure of its hollows and the loftiness of its rocks. The Ideas which it forces upon the mind are the sublime, the dreadful and the vast. Above is inaccessible altitude, below is horrible profundity.

His epithets were carefully and precisely chosen but by Jane Austen's time they would be well-worn clichés.

The entry for 25 July 1774 in Samuel Johnson's journal of a tour in north Wales. Add. MS 12070, ff. 4v–5.

Richard Graves

Five years after Samuel Johnson's visit to Hawkestone estate (see opposite), Richard Graves published his novel *Columella, or the Distressed Anchoret* (1779). Columella's park, described as being in the west of England, has many a parallel with Hawkestone and also with William Shenstone's garden at The Leasowes. Graves and Shenstone were close friends. The 'wild cataract…falling from a rock of prodigious height, shaded by a gloomy scene of old trees and wild shrubs' finds its place in many examples of this genre.

Gilbert White

Central to Gilbert White's *The Natural History of Selborne*, published in 1789, is a running history of his own garden. He was devoted to it. Between 1751 and 1767 he recorded his activities and observations by hand on the blank sheets of a 'garden Kalendar' and ensured that even in his absence someone else, usually his gardener, Thomas Hoar, who was with him for forty years, took over the task.

In 1767 White received some extremely useful printed forms designed by a fellow naturalist, Daines Barrington. An example of one of them, bearing White's entries, is illustrated here. Until his death in 1793 he thus maintained an orderly log of the natural phenomena of his Hampshire village and its environs, and of his work in his garden. (The poet Thomas Gray also began using these forms at the same time.)

The most minute particulars are noted; nothing was too small. We can smile at entries such as the one for 15 May 1788:

> Shaved my mongrel dog Rover and made use of his white hair in plaster for ceilings. His coat weighed four ounces.

and be cheered by the simple and evocative words that close the illustrated text 'Fritillaria blows'.

Above Pen-and-ink portrait of Gilbert White, probably made by Thomas Chapman, on the front flyleaf of a copy of Pope's translation of *The Iliad*. This and another small portrait elsewhere in this work are the only known likenesses of White. Add. MS 38877, f. 1.
Left Gilbert White's entries for the week of 6–12 April 1788 in his 'Naturalist's Journal'. Add. MS 31850, f. 52.

John Keats

To stand in the garden of Keats' house in Hampstead, north London, is to be reminded of a letter the poet wrote to his sister in the Spring of 1819:

> I ordered some bulbous roots for you at the Gardeners, and they sent me some but they were all in bud and could not be sent so I put them in the garden…

It was here, under the plum tree, sitting on a chair taken from the breakfast table, that he began the first draft of 'Ode to a Nightingale'.

THE FAT BOY AWAKE ON THIS OCCASION ONLY.

Charles Dickens

Notwithstanding the garden arbour's long history as a vestibule of dalliance and its fashionableness as a rustic adornment in villa gardens in the 1830s, Dickens had no illusions about it. Of the one illustrated here from his *Pickwick Papers* (first published in 1836) he said:

> There was a bower at the further end, with honeysuckle, jessamine and creeping plants – one of those sweet retreats which humane men erect for the accommodation of spiders.

In an address to a Gardeners' Benevolent Society dinner in 1852, chaired incidentally by the great gardener Joseph Paxton himself, he was, nevertheless, his usual charitable self:

> The wind that blows over the cottager's porch sweeps also over the grounds of the nobleman and…the gardener of the rich man, in developing and enhancing a fruitful flavour or a delightful scent, is in some sort the gardener of everybody else.

Above right R. W. Buss's idea of the arbour scene in the first edition of *Pickwick Papers* and (**left**) the re-working of it by Hablot Browne (Phiz) in later editions.
012273. ff. 3/1.
c.59.c.23, vol. i.

John and Jane Loudon

John Claudius Loudon (1783–1843) and his wife Jane may be little known, as names, to us today, but their influence on gardening was very big indeed. As a garden designer, Loudon favoured comfortably enclosed areas, which could be come across by surprise, where each feature revealed its worth and beauty, the basis for what is known as 'the gardenesque'.

With a strong social instinct, he produced designs for many free municipal parks, botanical gardens and cemeteries, at a time – in the 1830s and 1840s – when civic leaders in our increasingly crowded, troublesome and insanitary towns became aware of their importance. The design for his first park – that in Gravesend, which has since been completely built over – was made in 1836.

Loudon was the first horticultural journalist and he published prolifically. His wife, who produced nineteen horticultural books herself, established a trend with her *Gardening for Ladies* (1841).

Right Design for a villa residence, by J. C. Loudon, December 1830. 1899. h. 11. **Left** A page from Jane Loudon's *The Ladies' Flower-garden of Ornamental Perennials*, 2 vols, London, 1843–44. 722. l. 6.

DESIGN *for laying out 10 Acres of flat surface as a* VILLA RESIDENCE *the trees & shrubs arranged according to the* JUSSIEUEAN *System*   Plate VIII.

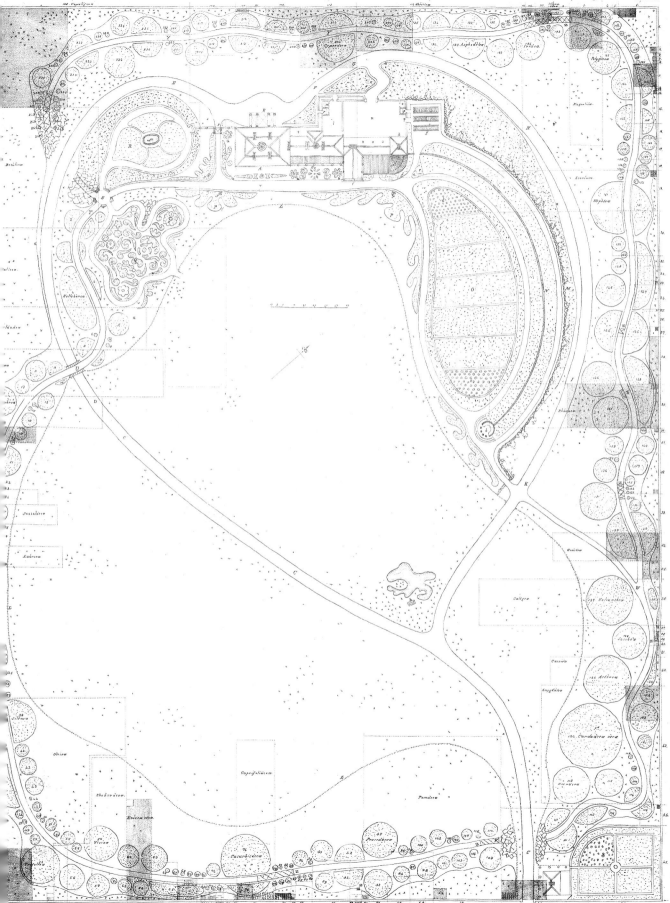

Designed by J.C. Loudon, drawn on stone by J. Robertson, printed by C. Hullmandel, and published by Longman & Co. & Treuttel & Wurtz London. Dec.r 1830.

Alfred Lord Tennyson

Shown here in Alfred Lord Tennyson's autograph hand are the last two verses of section twelve from his long dramatic poem *Maud* (published 1855). The whole poem – of twenty-eight sections – is a monodrama whose speaker is a man deranged by his passion for Maud to the point of madness, and the garden, playing a large part in the drama, reflects the theme. It is a garden of the subconscious where sexual and social tensions are played out in the fevered imagery:

> There has fallen a splendid tear
>   From the passion-flower at the gate.
> She is coming, my love, my dear;
>   She is coming, my life, my fate...

Below Tennyson's fair copy of two verses from *Maud* (written 1854; published 1855). Add. MS 45741, f. 279.
Left Julia Margaret Cameron's photographic image, published in 1875, of Maud. She places her subject, actually one of her own domestic staff, precisely in the poem's context. Tennyson Research Centre, Lincoln, by permission of Lincolnshire County Council.

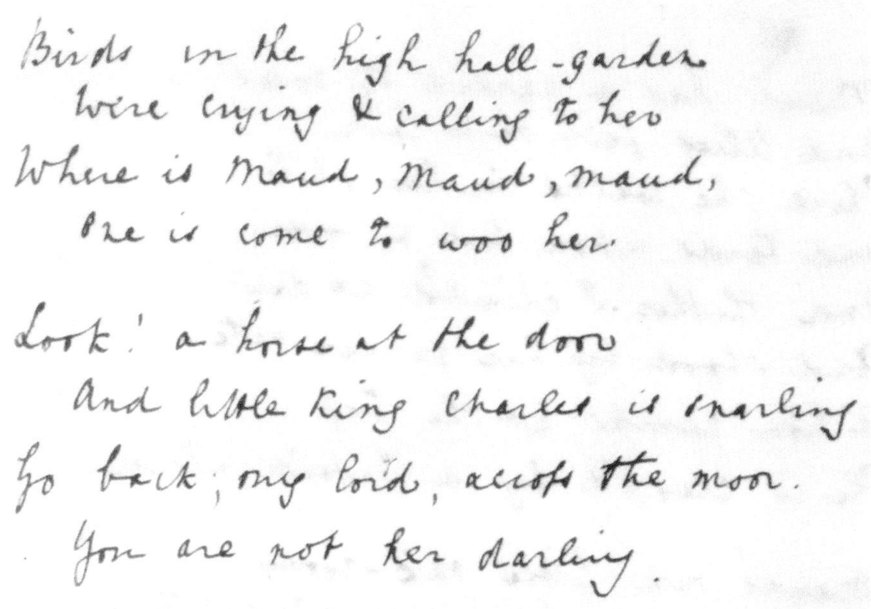
Birds in the high hall-garden
Were crying & calling to her
Where is Maud, Maud, Maud,
One is come to woo her.

Look! a horse at the door
And little King Charles is snarling
Go back, my lord, across the moor.
You are not her darling.

Edward Lear

In 1880 Edward Lear built his last home, the Villa Tennyson, in San Remo, with its terraced garden facing the Mediterranean Sea. Though not an ardent hands-on gardener, he had a particular attraction towards varieties of *Ipomoea*, having gathered seeds in India. In San Remo, he brought to their cultivation a scientific interest, having achieved much success in growing them.

The *Ipomoea* flower has a life span of about a day and this manifestation of transitoriness may account partly for its appeal to Lear, a man given – for all the delights of his whimsical humour – to profoundest melancholy.

Below Edward Lear's drawing of himself: 'Mr Lear a-watering of his flowers, April 24, 1871.' From *The Later Letters of Edward Lear*, ed. Lady Strachey, London, 1911. 010902. ff. 14.
Right The blue flower is *Ipomoea sagittifolia* and the white flower is *Ipomoea pandurata*. The others are varieties of *Convolvulus*. A plate from Jane Loudon's *The Ladies' Flower-Garden of Ornamental Perennials*, 2 vols, London, 1843–44. 722. l. 6.

Pl. 76.

1 *Convolvulus sepium Americanus*. _ 2 *Convolvulus reniformis*. _ 3 *Convolvulus Bryoniæfolia*.
4 *Ipomæa pandurata*. _ 5. *Ipomæa sagittifolia*.

Walter Crane

The Pre-Raphaelites, notable for their precision of detail, had a great influence on Walter Crane as a designer, and the world he created of rhythmically arranged organic forms, lent itself to stories of enchantment. He wrote his own stories and illustrated them himself with a view to teaching children to read by associating words with pictures.

Here we see three of his enchanted gardens. In his *Jack and the Beanstalk* of 1898 (first published in 1874) the familiar bold, leafy forms of William Morris's wallpaper designs are evident. The effects are more fragile in his *Floral Fantasy* of 1899; in this volume a series of garden flowers disport themselves in anthropomorphic forms. In 'The Selfish Giant', only the picture of the giant and the Christ-child in the tree is Crane's own. The story, published in 1888, is by Oscar Wilde.

Below Oscar Wilde's 'The Selfish Giant' published in *The Happy Prince and other stories*, 1888. The opening with an illustration by Crane. T. C. 4. a. 9.

The Selfish Giant.

The Selfish Giant.

EVERY afternoon, as they were coming from school, the children used to go and play in the Giant's garden.

It was a large lovely garden, with soft green grass. Here and there over the grass stood beautiful flowers like stars, and there were twelve peach-trees that in the spring-time broke out into delicate blossoms of pink and pearl, and in the autumn bore rich fruit. The birds sat on the trees and sang so sweetly that the children used to stop their games in order to listen to them. "How happy we are here!" they cried to each other.

45

Above Walter Crane's
*A Floral Fantasy in an
old English Garden*,
1899. The opening
pages. 11651. l. 47.
Left Crane's version of
Jack and the Beanstalk,
1898, with his own
illustrations. The closing
pages of the tale.
12809. w. 56.

Frances Hodgson Burnett

Frances Hodgson Burnett herself acknowledged the importance of a particular garden as the source for her book *The Secret Garden*, published in 1911. It was at Maytham Hall in Rolvenden, Kent, which she rented from 1898 until 1907. The walled orchard there was an abandoned wilderness entered by a wooden door in a low arched gateway. This she turned into a rose garden where she would write.

Transposed onto the Yorkshire moors, this is the garden discovered by Mary Lennox in Burnett's famous story. Mary – and this is part of her enlightenment – allows Dickon, a boy who lives nearby, to share her secret.

But there is another garden in the novel:

> The secret garden was not the only one Dickon worked in. Round the cottage on the moor there was a piece of ground enclosed by a low wall of rough stones…Dickon worked there planting or tending potatoes and cabbages, turnips and carrots and herbs for his mother…There were not only vegetables in this garden. Dickon had bought penny packages of flower seeds now and then and sown bright, sweet-scented things among gooseberry bushes and even cabbages and he grew borders of mignonette and pinks and pansies…

Neither garden goes beyond the bounds of reality and so neither can strictly be called a garden of enchantment, but they are both restorative, the secret garden offering a balm to a troubled mind and a cure to a crippled body. The cottage garden in that Edwardian twilight offered a reassuring, though naïve, glimpse, seen repeatedly in Helen Allingham's watercolours, of a comfortable England that was soon to be almost swept away.

Left Mary's discovery of the secret garden. An illustration by Charles Robinson for the first edition of the novel, 1911. 012809. aaa. 6.

Above 'The Clothes Basket', a watercolour of a Surrey cottage, by Helen Allingham from *The Cottage Homes of England* edited by Stewart Dick, 1909. 7815. p. 15.

Edward Thomas

In his untitled poem from 1915, Edward Thomas's image of a lost garden, delicate though it is, powerfully captures the plight of a generation. But it contains hope. Thomas himself was killed in battle in 1917 and is buried in Agny Military Cemetery in Pas-de-Calais, France.

For those at home, the sight of convalescent maimed soldiers in the grounds of our sanatoria – such as that at Craiglockhart where Wilfred Owen wrote some of his finest verse before returning to die at the front – was horror enough. Lawson Wood's sanitised sketch shown here hid much of the truth.

Above Preparatory sketch for a poster or book cover. Watercolour by Lawson Wood, c.1917. Egerton MS 3863, f. 51.
Right Autograph draft of an untitled poem, dated 1915, by Edward Thomas. Add. MS 44990, f. 46.

'The Nightingale' a pen, ink and wash drawing, dated 1933, by Arthur George Watts (1883–1935). Watts designed posters for London Underground and had a special aptitude for capturing suburban life. MS Deposit 10212.

Katherine Mansfield

Katherine Mansfield's short story *A Suburban Fairy Tale*, written in 1917 though not published until 1924, is an oddly disturbing tale of a plump middle-class couple obsessively occupied with eating. They provide for their diminutive child at the table but beyond that he is given scant regard and when he silently joins the hungry sparrows outside in 'the cold empty garden patch', they barely notice.

It is a tale of blunted sensibilities, of detachment. The garden here, with its 'grey frozen grass', is no garden of enchantment but a sterile little area touched neither by love nor by imagination.

Arthur Watts's drawing entitled 'The Nightingale', created for *Punch* in 1933, is a comic study in the same kind of disengagement.

AT LEAST COST

Crown Copyright Reserved

All Rights Reserved

HOW TO GROW FOOD

THE
GARDEN A.B.C.

APPROVED BY THE
HORTICULTURAL COMMISSIONER OF THE
MINISTRY OF AGRICULTURE

4D.

The Garden ABC, edited by
Alfred W. Yeo, Eastbourne,
1940. 07029. ff. 38.

Laurence Binyon

Between 1939 and 1945 those at home were urged to contribute
to the war effort by utilising their garden plots for food production.
Government departments issued little guides to good husbandry,
such as the one illustrated here.

It was a dark time, but the poem 'The Orchard' by Laurence Binyon
holds promise for the future, as Edward Thomas's poem did in 1915.
Binyon's lines for the fallen ('They shall grow not old, as we that are
left grow old…') are engraved on many a 'stony monument'. When
he died in 1943, the poem was found among his papers and
published by his widow in *The Burning of the Leaves*, 1944.

The Orchard

Almond, apple, and peach,
Walnut, cherry, plum,
Ash, chestnut, and beech,
And lime and sycamore
We have planted for days to come;

No stony monument
But growing, changing things,
Leaf, fruit, and honied scent,
Bloom that the bees explore,
Sprays where the bird sings.

In other Junes than ours
When the boughs spread and rise
Tall into leafy towers
To grace and guard this small
Corner of paradise;

When petals red and white
Resign to warming air,
Without speech or sight
From our hands they will fall
On happy voices there.

Permission to reproduce 'The Orchard' has been granted
by The Society of Authors as the Literary Representative
of the Estate of Laurence Binyon.

An Outside View of SISINGHERST CASTLE, in the COUNTY of KENT, dedicated to the Officers of the Militia Engraved from a Drawing taken on the Spot By an Officer 1760

Vita Sackville-West

Alluding to T. S. Eliot's image of the Waste Land, Vita Sackville-West valiantly proclaims her own intent in her poem 'The Garden':

> The land and not the waste land celebrate,
> The rich and hopeful land, the solvent land,
> Not some poor desert strewn with nibbled
>   bones…

Published in 1946, this was a rallying affirmation of purposeful recovery after the war's debilitating struggle. Her optimism and that of her husband Harold Nicolson had been manifest in their acquisition of Sissinghurst Castle in Kent in 1930, for the seven-acre estate was then virtually a waste land itself, filled with assorted rubbish entangled with bindweed and wire netting that took three years to clear.

By dint of sheer labour, an exquisite garden of formal lines softened by a romantic profusion of planting emerged. And to carry the spirit of achievement, painfully won, into the post-war years, they began the creation of the great White Garden in 1949.

The White Garden at Sissinghurst, National Trust. **Above** An outside view of Sissinghurst Castle, engraved from a drawing taken on the spot by an officer, 1760. Nearly all the buildings shown were pulled down or tumbled down in the nineteenth century. K. Top. xviii. 52. 2. a.

Philip Larkin

Philip Larkin became librarian of the Brynmor Jones Library at the University of Hull in 1955, and, living snugly as a tenant at the top of a three-storied house that faced a park, he had for the next nineteen years little reason to think of gardening. The sale of the house in 1974, however, forced his hand: with no enthusiasm whatsoever, he made his first purchase of a home of his own and acquired an ugly 1950s dwelling close to the University. 'It has a huge garden', he wrote, '– not a lovely wilderness (though it soon will be) – a long strip between wire fences – oh God, oh God – I'm "taking over" the vendors' Qualcast [lawnmower].'

He never acquired an interest in the garden and, significantly, placed his fireside chair with its back to it. He sometimes let the grass grow high and quite impractically tried to cut it down in a wet condition. It was in these circumstances that the incident described in his poem 'The Mower', printed here, took place. A draft of the poem is dated 12 June 1979.

The incident affected him deeply. He was always compassionate towards animals (on his death in 1985 he left half his estate to the RSPCA) but equally important were his own apprehensions of mortality. It is notable that in 'The Mower', perceived as 'the Grim Reaper', he looks back to Andrew Marvell, another Hull poet. Marvell wrote a sequence of four Mower Poems, all published in 1681. Larkin's poem has affinities with the last of them, 'The Mower's Song':

> …flow'rs, and grass, and I and all
> Will in one common ruin fall…

From this point in time the lawnmower became Larkin's bête noire. Correspondence, starting in October 1979, survives of his two-year struggle with his motor-mower dealer to replace his machine with one that worked satisfactorily and then to replace that with a third. It makes melancholy reading.

The Mower

The mower stalled, twice; kneeling, I found
A hedgehog jammed up against the blades,
Killed. It had been in the long grass.

I had seen it before, and even fed it, once.
Now I had mauled its unobtrusive world
Unmendably. Burial was no help:

Next morning I got up and it did not.
The first day after a death, the new absence
Is always the same; we should be careful

Of each other, we should be kind
While there is still time.

Top 'The Mower' was first published in *Humberside* (Hull Literary
Club Magazine), Autumn, 1979. Copyright the Estate of Philip
Larkin, by kind permission of Faber and Faber Ltd.
Above Photograph of a hedgehog taken by Philip Larkin in his own
garden, n.d. Copyright the Estate of Philip Larkin, by permission of
The Society of Authors as the Literary Representatives of the Estate
of Philip Larkin. Thanks to Hull University Archives.

Sir Michael Tippett

The libretto of Sir Michael Tippett's third opera, *The Knot Garden* (first performed at Covent Garden in 1970), was written by him. It is about the troubled relationships of six people into whose lives comes a retired psychoanalyst called Mangus. He stages a kind of group therapy in which private fantasies come to the surface.

The garden in which the whole action is set goes beyond the Tudor knot garden, symbolic enough in itself, to the enclosed garden of *Le Roman de la Rose*, the Garden of Pleasure, for in the opera we also have lovers, a fountain and music. Here, however, it is turned on its head: instead of the harmony of love we are presented with the discord of love.

Autograph draft of part of the libretto to Tippett's *The Knot Garden*, taken from one of his notebooks. Thea is described elsewhere in the manuscript as 'a passionate gardener'. Add. MS 72041, f. 58v. Reproduced by kind permission of Schott and Co. Limited.

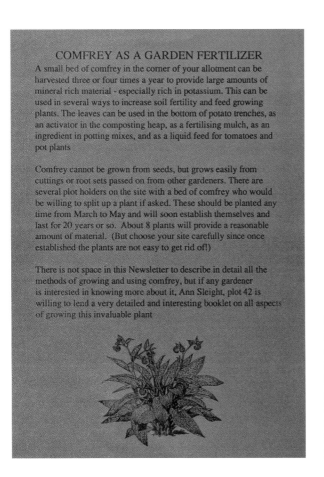

COMFREY AS A GARDEN FERTILIZER

A small bed of comfrey in the corner of your allotment can be harvested three or four times a year to provide large amounts of mineral rich material - especially rich in potassium. This can be used in several ways to increase soil fertility and feed growing plants. The leaves can be used in the bottom of potato trenches, as an activator in the composting heap, as a fertilising mulch, as an ingredient in potting mixes, and as a liquid feed for tomatoes and pot plants.

Comfrey cannot be grown from seeds, but grows easily from cuttings or root sets passed on from other gardeners. There are several plot holders on the site with a bed of comfrey who would be willing to split up a plant if asked. These should be planted any time from March to May and will soon establish themselves and last for 20 years or so. About 8 plants will provide a reasonable amount of material. (But choose your site carefully since once established the plants are not easy to get rid of!)

There is not space in this Newsletter to describe in detail all the methods of growing and using comfrey, but if any gardener is interested in knowing more about it, Ann Sleight, plot 42 is willing to lend a very detailed and interesting booklet on all aspects of growing this invaluable plant

Left From *The Plot*, the Skircoat Green Allotment Association Newsletter, no. 11, Spring 1991, by kind permission of the association. According to a herbal of 1578, 'the rootes of comfery… healeth all inwarde woundes and burstings'. ZK. 9. a. 981.

Melvyn Bragg

Melvyn Bragg's novel *Crystal Rooms* (1992) presents us with a picture of a fractured society, our own, where the protagonist, a parliamentary candidate out canvassing, is shamed into guilt by the social divisions he sees and by the lack of 'joy on the streets'. However, he comes upon something unexpected:

> …he stopped dead at the sight which met him. It was like a smile, it was like a little Eden of thoughtful pleasure: a swathe of allotments. A quilted spread of ground descending an easy slope to the railway lines. Fences marked out individual stakes. Paths pottered through the site like the twisting streets of medieval hill towns. Shocks of blooms – chrysanthemums, blowsy peonies – sat beside neatly drilled lines of vegetables…To each plot of land, it seemed to Nicholas, there was a man, digging, tying, mending, cultivating, dreaming.

Drawn into conversation by plot holders, he finds comfort and a sense of union, above all, a warmth in the contact, 'almost body warmth'. When darkness falls, he leaves with regret, for in this encounter he has found peace.

Detail from Walter Crane's
*A Floral Fantasy in an old
English Garden*, 1899.
11651. l. 47.

Title page Wheelbarrow from Revd. C. A.
Johns, *Gardening for Children*, 1848.
7055.a.32

The author, Roger Evans, was formerly a curator
of Literary Manuscripts at The British Library.

He would like to acknowledge the assistance
of Chris Fletcher, Frances Harris, Peter Barber,
Georgina Difford and Roger Christian in
compiling this book.

The Writer in the Garden
An exhibition at The British Library
5 November 2004 – 10 April 2005
Curated by Chris Fletcher, Frances Harris, Sally
Brown, Peter Barber and Roger Evans with the
assistance of Janet Benoy, Alan Sterenberg and
Geraldine Kenny.

Supported by the John S. Cohen Foundation
and the Basil Samuel Foundation

First published 2004 by
The British Library
96 Euston Road
London NW1 2DB

British Library Cataloguing-in-Publication Data
A catalogue record for this book is
available from The British Library

ISBN 0 7123 4889 1

Designed by The British Library
Corporate Design Office
Printed in England by Cambridge
University Press